Ulysses S. Grant

MILITARY LEADERS OF THE CIVIL WAR

Don McLeese

Rourke
Publishing LLC
Vero Beach, Florida 32964

www.rourkepublishing.com

PHOTO CREDITS: ©Armentrout pgs 6/7, 8/9, 10/11
All other images from the Library of Congress

Title page: A photograph of General Ulysses S. Grant

Editor: Frank Sloan

Cover and page design by Nicola Stratford

Library of Congress Cataloging-in-Publication Data

McLeese, Don.
  Ulysses S. Grant / Don McLeese.
     p. cm. -- (Military leaders of the civil war)
  Includes index.
  ISBN 1-59515-475-2 (hardcover)
 1. Grant, Ulysses S. (Ulysses Simpson), 1822-1885--Juvenile literature. 2.
Generals--United States--Biography--Juvenile literature. 3. United States.
Army--Biography--Juvenile literature. 4. United States--History--Civil War,
1861-1865--Campaigns--Juvenile literature. 5. Presidents--United
States--Biography--Juvenile literature. I. Title.
  E672.M1555 2006
  973.8'2'092--dc22

                            2005010979

Printed in the USA

Rourke Publishing
1-800-394-7055
www.rourkepublishing.com
sales@rourkepublishing.com
Post Office Box 3328, Vero Beach, FL 32964

Table of Contents

~

The General
Who Won the War

~

As the head of the **Union** army during the Civil War, Ulysses S. Grant was the most famous **general** of the North. The North defeated the South during the war, so Grant was the winning general. He defeated the Southern **Confederate** army that was led by Robert E. Lee.

Grant was a hero after the war. Four years after the Civil War ended, he was elected president of the United States. He was the 18th person elected to the highest office in the country. He was president from 1869 to 1877. He was not considered a great president. But he is remembered as a great general.

A picture of Grant against a background that shows scenes of his life, from his West Point days to the Confederate surrender that ended the Civil War

A modern photograph of the house where Grant was born in Point Pleasant, Ohio

Hiram Was His Name

～

Ulysses was Grant's middle name when he was a boy. He was born on April 27, 1822. His parents named their baby Hiram Ulysses Grant. He was the first child in the family. He later had two brothers and three sisters.

Grant's parents lived in Point Pleasant, Ohio, near the Ohio River. His father's name was Jesse Root Grant. His mother's name was Hannah Simpson Grant. They had moved from Pennsylvania west to Ohio.

Ulysses: This was the name of a great leader and war hero thousands of years ago in Greece. The name is pronounced "You LISS eez."

7

"Useless"

～

Even though his real first name was Hiram, the family called him by his middle name, Ulysses. Because it was an unusual name, other kids made fun of him. He was very small and very quiet, without many friends. Instead of saying his name the correct way, the other kids called him "useless." Nobody ever thought this small boy would grow up to be one of the most famous men in America!

A modern-day photograph of the house in Georgetown, Ohio, where Grant's family lived

Young Grant attended school at this building in Georgetown.

School Days

~

Until he was 14, Ulysses went to school in Georgetown, Ohio. This was a small town where his parents had moved when he was one year old. He liked reading a lot, and he was very good with numbers, but he wasn't one of the best students. He enjoyed working on his family's farm. He liked horses best of all. He thought that when he grew up he might become a farmer.

Horses: Ulysses later wrote of his work on the farm, "I did all the work done with the horses."

A Mistake in His Name

~

When Ulysses was 16, his father wanted him to go to the United States **Military** Academy in West Point, New York. He could go to college there for free and then would become an officer in the army.

Those who go to West Point need a letter from their **congressman** saying that they should be let in. The congressman from Ohio wrote the letter, but he didn't know that Ulysses's real first name was Hiram. He thought it was Ulysses, since that's what everybody called him.

When Ulysses was admitted, he didn't let anyone know about the mistake. He thought other students might tease him about the name Hiram Ulysses Grant. Instead, Ulysses put his name down as Ulysses S. Grant. Those **initials** were U.S., like United States.

Grant's Middle Name: Some books give his name as Ulysses Simpson Grant. Simpson was his mother's last name before she married his father.

A view of West Point from the Hudson River

*At West Point Grant learned the skills he
needed to become a great soldier and leader.*

At West Point

~

Ulysses had never wanted to be a **soldier**, and he still wasn't a very good student. But his father made him go to West Point in 1839. He didn't like it there. He often got into trouble for breaking the many rules. When you broke a rule, you got a mark, called a **demerit**, next to your name. Ulysses had a lot more demerits than most of the students.

When Grant finished at West Point in 1843, his grades put him right in the middle of his class. He was ranked 21st out of 39 students.

Demerits: A demerit is the opposite of merit. Merit means that you deserve something good. A demerit shows that you have done something bad.

In the Army

~

The Mexican War: This was fought between the United States and Mexico from 1846 to 1848. At the time, land that is now Texas and California was part of Mexico. Ulysses called it a "wicked war."

Ulysses had wanted to be a college teacher. But everyone who went to West Point had to serve in the army after school. So instead of being a teacher, Ulysses became a soldier. He was sent south to Missouri and Louisiana.

When the Mexican War started in 1846, Grant went to Texas to fight in it. He thought it was bad to be at war with Mexico. He even thought about leaving the army. Even so, Grant fought bravely and was honored for it.

16

Grant is shown here at the capture of Mexico City during the Mexican War.

Grant's wife, the former Julia Dent

Married to Julia

~

When Ulysses was at West Point, he shared a room with Frederick Dent. Frederick's family lived near St. Louis. He had a sister named Julia. Frederick told his roommate and sister about each other.

When the army sent Ulysses to Missouri, he visited the Dent family. He and Julia fell in love. After he returned from the Mexican War in 1848, they were married.

College roommates: When students go to college, they often share a room with someone they've never met before. By living together, the roommates sometimes become very good friends.

19

A Loving Family

~

Ulysses and Julia loved each other very much. They soon had four children, three boys and a girl. When the army sent Ulysses west to California in 1853, he had to leave his family behind. The trip would be dangerous and cost too much money.

A formal portrait of Grant, his four children, and Mrs. Grant

20

A photograph of the Grants and their son, Jesse

Ulysses hated being apart from his family. He was very lonely and missed them very much. In 1854, he left the army and came back to live with his family in St. Louis.

The Grant farm, near St. Louis, Missouri

Tough Times

~

Though Ulysses loved being back with his family, the next six years were tough. He had many jobs and wasn't very good at any of them. He had once wanted to be a farmer. But when Julia's father bought them a farm near St. Louis, Ulysses had trouble selling crops. He also got very sick.

Ulysses later went to work for a company that rented houses, but he wasn't very good there either. He was often late for work and got into trouble.

Grant's father had opened a store that sold leather goods in Galena, Illinois. Ulysses and his family moved to Galena in 1860, and he went to work at the store. He didn't really like working in a store, but he had to do something to make money.

23

Leather goods: Ever since Ulysses was a young boy in Ohio, his father had worked with leather. Leather comes from the skin of a cow and is used to make belts, shoes, jackets, and other things.

Back to War

~

In 1861, the Civil War started between the Northern states and those in the South. The North wanted to make it against the law to have **slaves**. A slave is a person owned by another person. The South had many slaves. When the Southern states tried to leave the United States to form the Confederate States of America, the North said they couldn't leave. The war would decide whether the United States would be one country or two.

Grant fought in the Battle of Shiloh in Tennessee in April of 1862.

Ulysses wanted to serve his country in time of war, so he returned to the army. He showed himself to be a good leader, so he became a brigadier general, leading the **troops** in Illinois.

This photograph shows Grant at his headquarters in City Point, Virginia,

*Grant's victory at the Battle of Vicksburg in
1863 helped weaken the Confederate forces.*

Head of the Army

~

Ulysses was such a strong leader and brave fighter that his U.S. initials gave him a new nickname: "Unconditional **Surrender**." This meant that he wouldn't stop fighting until the other side completely gave up. President Abraham Lincoln said of him, "I can't spare this man. He fights."

Grant won some important battles, including Vicksburg, in the first few years of the war. In 1864, President Lincoln made him head of the entire Union army. Grant led more than 500,000 soldiers. Robert E. Lee, head of the Southern army, didn't have nearly as many troops.

The South fought hard but the North was stronger. On April 9, 1865, Lee surrendered to Grant, and the war was over.

*Grant takes the oath of office as
president at his 1869 inauguration.*

28

A Big Hero

~

As head of the winning army, Grant was very popular. In 1868, he was elected president. He was president until 1877. He wasn't nearly as good at leading the country as he had been at leading the army. But even those who didn't think he was a good president remembered him as a great general.

Ulysses S. Grant died on July 23, 1885.

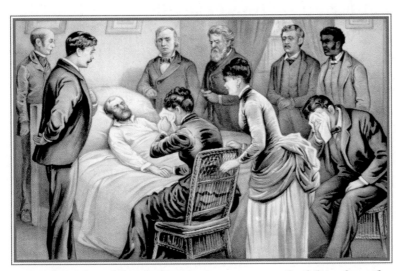

On his deathbed Grant is surrounded his family.

29

Important Dates to Remember

1822   Hiram Ulysses Grant is born.

1839   Grant is admitted to West Point as
"Ulysses S. Grant."

1843   Grant finishes at West Point and is sent to Missouri
by the army.

1846   The army sends Ulysses to fight in the Mexican War.

1848   Ulysses marries Julia Dent.

1854   Ulysses leaves the army.

1861   The Civil War starts and Ulysses returns to the army.

1864   President Abraham Lincoln names General Grant
head of the Union army.

1865   The North wins the Civil War when Robert E. Lee
surrenders to Grant.

1868   Grant is elected president.

1885   Ulysses S. Grant dies.

Glossary

Confederate (kon FED ur et) — a person, state, or soldier on the Southern side in the Civil War

congressman (KON gress man) — a member of congress (back then, they were all men)

demerit (deh MAIR it) — a mark against someone who has broken a rule

general (JEN ur ul) — the highest rank in the military

initials (ih NIH shuhlz) — first letters: your initials are the first letters of your first, middle, and last names

military (MILL ih TARE ee) — the armed forces

slaves (SLAYVZ) — people who are owned by another person

soldier (SOHL jer) — someone who serves in the military

surrender (sir REND der) — give up

troops (TRUUPS) — soldiers

Union (YOON yun) — the Northern side in the Civil War

Index

Further Reading

Carter, E.J., *Ulysses S. Grant* (American War Biographies), Heinemann, 2004.

O'Shea, Tim. *Ulysses S. Grant* (Famous Figures of the Civil War Era),
   Chelsea House, 2001.

Schulman, Michael A. *Ulysses S. Grant* (United States Presidents),
   Enslow Publishers, 2004.

Websites To Visit

http://empirenet.com/~ulysses/

http://www.americancivilwar.com/north/grant.html

http://www.lib.siu.edu/projects/usgrant/grant2.htm

About The Author

Don McLeese is an associate professor of journalism at the University of Iowa. He has won many awards for his journalism, and his work has appeared in numerous newspapers and magazines. He has frequently contributed to the World Book Encyclopedia and has written many books for young readers. He lives with his wife and two daughters in West Des Moines, Iowa.